animal babies
in seas

KINGFISHER

Kingfisher Publications Plc
New Penderel House
283–288 High Holborn
London WC1V 7HZ
www.kingfisherpub.com

First published by Kingfisher Publications Plc 2006
10 9 8 7 6 5 4 3 2 1

1TR/1105/TWP/SGCH(SGCH)/150STORA/C

Copyright © Kingfisher Publications Plc 2006

A CIP catalogue record for this book
is available from the British Library.

ISBN-13: 978 0 7534 1303 6
ISBN-10: 0 7534 1303 5

Author: Sue Nicholson
Senior Editor: Carron Brown
Designer: Joanne Brown
Proofreader: Sheila Clewley
Picture Research Manager: Cee Weston-Baker
DTP Co-ordinator: Catherine Hibbert
Senior Production Controller: Lindsey Scott

Printed in Singapore

animal babies

in seas

I am orange with a white stripe around my head. I flap my fins to help me swim.

Who is my mummy?

My mummy is
a clownfish and
I am her fry.

We live on a
coral reef. There
are many colourful
places to hide.

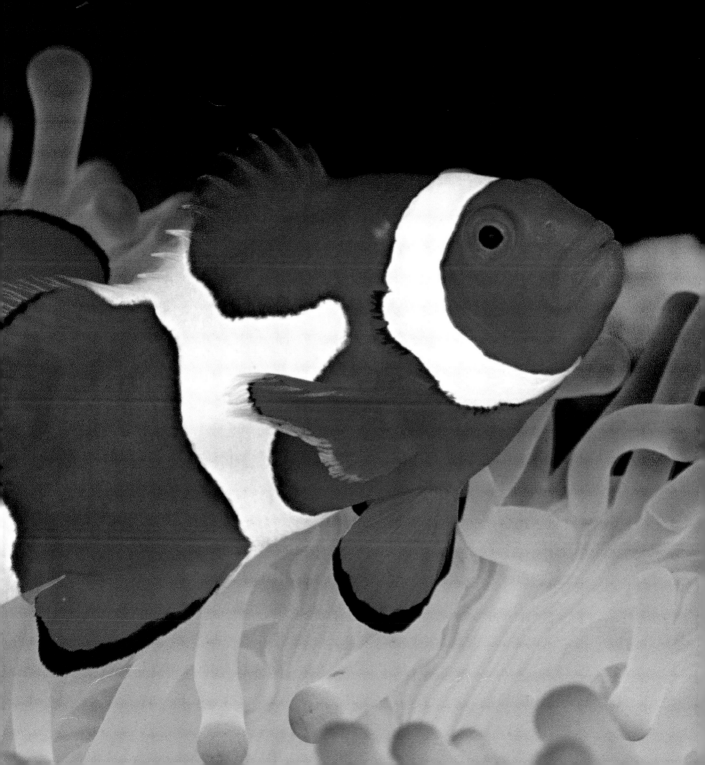

I have **soft**, speckled feathers and my **beak** has a black tip. I sleep in a grassy **nest**.

Who is my mummy?

My mummy is an Arctic tern and I am her chick.

I eat little fish caught by my mummy. Soon I will learn to fly and catch my own food.

I have a small, round head and tiny ears. My sleek, thick fur keeps me warm in the water.

Who is my mummy?

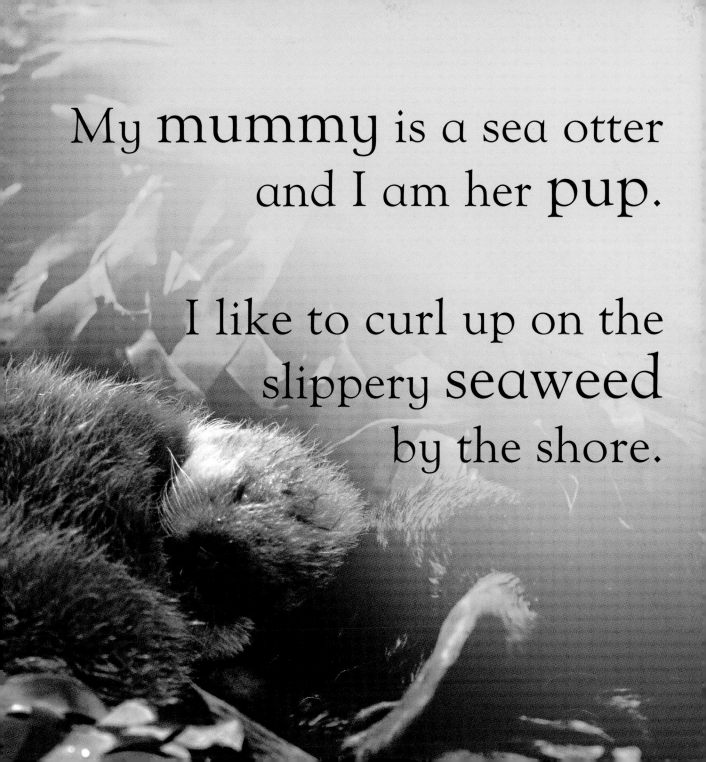

My mummy is a sea otter and I am her pup.

I like to curl up on the slippery seaweed by the shore.

I have smooth, grey skin and a wide, smiling mouth. I love to splash and leap through waves.

Who is my mummy?

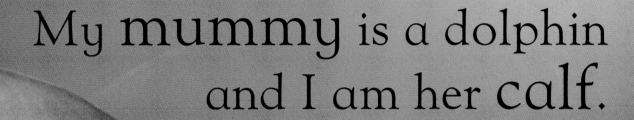

My mummy is a dolphin
and I am her calf.

I swim close to
my mummy so
I feel safe.

I am covered in soft, grey feathers. They keep me warm in the ice and snow.

Who is my mummy?

My **mummy** is an Adélie penguin and I am her **chick**.

I will soon have small, **smooth** feathers like my mummy's.

I have big, brown eyes, and a shiny, black nose. My whiskers are long and prickly.

Who is my mummy?

My mummy is a sea lion and I am her pup.

Sometimes, we like to scramble out of the sea to take a nap on the sand.

I have **rough** skin and will grow very **big**. I like to poke my head right out of the water.

Who is my mummy?

My mummy is a whale
and I am her calf.

We have to swim
up to the sea's
surface to take
a big breath
of air.

Additional Information

Two-thirds of the earth's surface is covered in oceans and seas, and they are full of life. The animals in this book live all over the world: clownfish live in the Coral sea; Arctic terns live in northern Europe and North America in summer and the Antarctic in winter; sea otters can be found along the shores of the Pacific ocean; bottlenose dolphins can be found in warm and tropical seas worldwide; Adélie penguins live only in the Antarctic; sea lions swim in the Indian and Pacific oceans around Australia; and humpback whales live in both polar and tropical waters around the world.

Acknowledgements

The publisher would like to thank the following for permission to reproduce their material. Every care has been taken to trace copyright holders. However, if there have been unintentional omissions or failure to trace copyright holders, we apologize and will, if informed, endeavour to make corrections in any future edition.

Cover: Frank Lane Picture Agency/Brigitte Wilms/Minden Pictures; Half-title: Photolibrary.com; Title page: Frank Lane Picture Agency/Flip Nicklin/Minden Pictures; Clownfish 1: Frank Lane Picture Agency/Brigitte Wilms/Minden Pictures; Clownfish 2: Frank Lane Picture Agency/Brigitte Wilms/Minden Pictures; Arctic tern 1: Corbis/Hans Dieter Brandl/Frank Lane Picture Agency; Arctic tern 2: Corbis/Jonathan Blair; Sea otter 1: Frank Lane Picture Agency/Tim Fitzharris/Minden Pictures; Sea otter 2: Photolibrary.com/Daniel Cox; Dolphin 1: Tom & Pat Leeson/ardea.com; Dolphin 2: Frank Lane Picture Agency/Flip Nicklin/Minden Pictures; Adélie penguin 1: Frank Lane Picture Agency/Frans Lanting/Minden Pictures; Adélie penguin 2: Corbis/Tim Davis; Sea lion 1: Photolibrary.com; Sea lion 2: Photolibrary.com/Tom Ulrich; Humpback whale 1: Seapics.com/Masa Ushioda; Humpback whale 2: Seapics.com/Doug Perrine